MW00856227

Many Americans likely know the Reverend Minister Louis Farrakhan founded the Nation of Islam. But do they know he's also a farmer? Farrakhan received more than $317,000 in federal farm subsidies and commodities loans at his home address in Hyde Park, Chicago during a sixteen-year period.

The subsidies were granted to a charity called the Three Year Economic Saving Program, which then, allegedly, distributed the funds to a 1,500-acre farm based in Georgia called "Muhammad Farms." The trouble is, the Three Year Economic Saving Program might not be a real charity – in 2014, the Cincinnati office of the Internal Revenue Service didn't have a record of it. The Illinois Secretary of State listed the Saving Program as "not in good standing." What's more, the Illinois Attorney General's office, which oversees the state's 501(c)(3) charities, in 2014, had no record of a charity registered with that name. And yet government checks flowed to Farrakhan, not in Georgia, of course, but at his home address in Chicago.

This is but one sadly typical illustration of the reach and perfidy of what has become popularly known as "the swamp."

"The swamp" is not just how we refer to Washington when the party we despise controls the levers of government. Nor is it merely a snarky designation for that generally disliked Mid-Atlantic wasteland known as the D.C. Beltway zone (despite the myth, Washington was not founded atop a drained swamp).

In America today, "the swamp" is a real thing: a permanent government within our government that will outlast this administration and the next one and the one after that. It has a massive architecture that can be measured. It is composed of tens of thousands of individuals – many of whom operate well outside the confines of Washington, D.C. And it is not just government employees. It is also the thousands of lobbyists working to keep

The administrative state's costly interventions into the daily lives of American citizens far outweigh its purported benefits.

pet projects funded, the thousands of rent-seeking private citizens who practice their own form of income redistribution by gobbling up tax dollars through federal subsidies, and the thousands of private-sector employees hired as independent contractors to do work the American people never asked for.

The larger the swamp grows, the more it entangles and imperils our everyday lives.

Americans are rightly suspicious. They know unfairness when they see it. But few Americans are aware just how far the tentacles of the swamp have spread, and just how tight a grip the swamp has on their everyday lives. While the idea of draining the swamp may seem to be a new one, it has a storied American history – which makes it all the more shocking that it has never been accomplished.

Indeed, Americans have loathed the swamp since long before President Donald Trump targeted it in his successful 2016 campaign. In fact, the slogan "drain the swamp" has a long and, surprisingly, bipartisan history. In 1983, Ronald Reagan pledged to drain the swamp, saying to constituents: "sometimes it is difficult to remember that you didn't send us to Washington to feed the alligators, you sent us to drain the swamp." Unfortunately, the alligators were still being fed by the time Senate Minority Leader Nancy Pelosi made the same promise in 2007, pledging to "break the link between lobbyists and legislation."

But just what is the swamp, and where did it come from? In technical terms, "the swamp" is perhaps best described as America's administrative state: a broad, unelected federal bureaucracy conceived by Progressives and willed into existence with the New Deal reforms. The administrative state technically falls under the purview of the executive branch, but today's administrative agencies function autonomously with little to no oversight or accountability to the presidency – or the American people.

The Left views the administrative state as a professional technocrat class that competently manages various federal programs for the benefit of the public. In the Left's view, the people, unable to help themselves, must be constantly taken care of by the federal government.

The Right argues that our elected officials have delegated far too much power to these agencies, that they operate with less-than-scientific efficiency, and that the administrative state's costly interventions into the daily lives of American citizens far outweigh its purported benefits.

OpenTheBooks fact checked the promises from both sides and conducted a full-scale investigation to reveal the size, scope, and effectiveness of this federal bureaucracy. We audited all publicly disclosed government salaries and bonuses for the 2016 fiscal year.

We learned what exactly it is they do, where they work, and how much they make.

We literally mapped the swamp. And the results were deeply alarming.

The current state of America's bureaucracy is unconscionably expensive. In 2016, there were 1.97 million civil service employees in the executive agencies (plus the U.S. Post Office), at a total cash cost of $136 billion. Federal bureaucrats are paid 1.1 million dollars every minute, $65.6 million every hour, and over half a billion dollars per day – and that's just cash compensation. This, by the way, is not counting the Department of Defense and our active military – one of the few expenditures that most Americans actually agree is essential to the security and wellbeing of our nation.

Many American workers spend their entire careers trying to earn six figures – indeed only 8 percent of Americans make $100,000 a year. In the swamp, however, six figures can be the norm. We found that $100,000 represents a kind of "minimum wage" for federal employees. There are 78 agencies where the average salary is $100,000 or more. Around 25 percent of federal employees make six figures – three times the percentage of private-sector workers. And the number of highly compensated federal employees is only growing. Between fiscal years 2010 and 2016, the number of federal employees making $200,000 or more increased by 165 percent. Our analysis showed that more than 406,000 federal employees earned six-figure incomes in 2016, while 30,000 rank-and-file federal employees received more than $190,823, out-earning each of the 50 state governors.

Federal bureaucrats are paid 1.1 million dollars every minute, $65.6 million every hour, and over half a billion dollars per day – and that's just cash compensation.

It is not just big salaries that make these federal employees so pricey – taxpayers also pay for lucrative perks like weeks of paid time off, performance bonuses, and padded retirement pensions. On average, federal employees receive 10 federal holidays, 13 sick days, and 20 vacation days per year. Compare that to the average 10 days of paid-time-off that private sector American workers receive. These benefits, which far exceed those offered in the private sector, cost taxpayers $22.6 billion annually.

On top of overly generous vacation time, the federal government pays out $1.5 billion in big bonuses every year. In 2016, there were more than 330,000 disclosed federal bonuses, but the largest bonus in the federal government ($141,525) didn't go to a doctor researching a cure for cancer or a rocket scientist helping us to reestablish dominance in space. Instead, it went to an HR Manager who's in charge of payroll at a small federal agency in San Francisco, California, called Presidio Trust. In fact, Presidio Trust – a needless agency about which we'll learn more later – awarded 3 of the 4 biggest bonuses in 2016.

All told, the federal workforce contains 579 job titles ranging from "Book Binding" to "Zoology." The scope for malfeasance is vast. But even legitimate jobs are sources of major waste. There are more than 35,000 lawyers in the administrative state. Yet just one-third of those lawyers work at the Department of Justice. The majority of these taxpayer-funded attorneys are dispersed across 90 agencies defending regulations rather than fighting crime and criminals. If the average American's life feels more burdened by regulation than ever before, there's a good reason for that. The army of lawyers in the employ of the federal government assures that no aspect of American life is untouched by the swamp's appendages.

Should the federal government reassess its payroll priorities? Is it necessary to maintain such an expansive and costly bureaucracy? Does a large and widespread federal workforce facilitate good government? The answers, after our study, are clear. Select case studies of governmental overreach in specific departments will make this even more apparent.

The EPA: Murky Waters

Elizabeth Southerland – who until August 2017 was the director of science and technology in the Environmental Protection Agency's Office of Water – might be the most famous EPA employee not named Scott Pruitt. In 2017, she made headlines for resigning from the EPA in protest over the way the Trump administration, under new director Pruitt, was "seriously weakening the EPA's mission by vigorously pursuing an industry deregulation approach and defunding implementation of environmental programs." Her public resignation, which decried "major budget cuts" that were not yet law, was lauded by the media as an example of a principled government employee standing up for her beliefs.

What the reporting failed to mention was that Southerland was one of the EPA's – and the federal government's – highest paid employees. In 2016, she earned a salary of $185,100, plus a bonus of $64,155, meaning her total government income exceeded Vice President Joe Biden's by nearly $20,000. Furthermore, Southerland's principled stand was anything but. In fact, she was eligible for a government pension, which allowed her to have her cake and eat it too. Rather than be thankful to the American people for the years of over-pay she received, Southerland rudely waltzed out the door with a cushy pension, too. Southerland is the true representation of the administrative state: exceedingly well-paid, entrenched, and infatuated with her singular ability to conduct the business of government.

This mentality is widespread throughout the administrative state. The EPA is a particular source of harmful bloat. Not only do its employees take home typically large salaries, they enjoy perks beyond any reasonable measure. Over a nine-year period, the agency spent $92 million on furniture alone. But while expensive office chairs are offensive enough, they don't touch the average American in the way some EPA programs do. Consider just one example of EPA overreach: the EPA has spent over $715 million on its "Criminal Enforcement Division." This staggering budget

---

The army of lawyers in the employ of the federal government assures that no aspect of American life is untouched by the swamp's appendages.

---

includes 200 special agents, armed with guns, ammunition, and military-grade equipment. It is hard to imagine why these agents would need such equipment, and harder still to fathom how it could cost so much.

All this would be easier to swallow if the EPA were not such a meddlesome organization. Take the case of John Duarte, a fourth-generation farmer who oversees 450 acres of a family farm in Northern California. In 2012, Duarte was accused by the EPA and Army Corps of Engineers of damaging wetland features on his property. The bill from the government in fines and restoration fees totaled $30 million. Duarte's crime? Tilling his own land. The EPA alleged that he had violated the Clean Water Act, which regulates tributaries that flow into larger bodies of water. Duarte's bad fortune – that wetlands on his property flowed into a larger body – resulted in the federal government requiring a permit before Duarte could cultivate land he had owned for decades. Such a permitting process can take years and includes conducting studies at the owner's expense. When Duarte failed to meet the EPA's unreasonable standards, he was targeted with an outrageous fine. Rather than litigate the injustice, he chose the sensible option of settling with the government for $1.1 million.

While the EPA was targeting family farmers like Duarte, the agency simultaneously employed 168 economists with salaries totaling $18.9 million to study "the application of the principles of economics to the study of how environmental and natural resources are developed and managed." If the EPA were more efficient, perhaps it wouldn't need to fine small-scale farmers tens of millions of dollars to fund itself.

THE VA: ANYTHING BUT CARE

In 2014, a courageous whistleblower named Dr. Sam Foote brought national attention to a "cook the books" wait-time bonus scandal at the Phoenix Veterans Affairs facility. At that facility alone, up to 40 veterans died while waiting to see a doctor and up to 1,300 veterans had to wait up to six months for an appointment – the average wait-time was 115 days.

And while veterans were waiting to see a doctor, the official books showed no wait-times at all. Though it started in Phoenix, the scandal spread nationwide, revealing similar issues at VA facilities across the country. During a ten-year period, more than 1,000 veterans died waiting to see a doctor, and many calls to the VA's suicide hotline were answered by an automated voicemail service. While even one veteran's needless death is an outrage, the VA's behavior during the scandal makes the situation even more appalling.

While veterans were suffering at the hands of a broken bureaucratic machine, the VA doled out tens of thousands of undeserved performance bonuses: $150 million per year. At the peak of the scandal, the U.S. House of Representatives voted 426–0 to end the practice of VA bonuses through 2016, but the Senate never took up the legislation. Yet during and after the worst scandal in Veterans Affairs history, the VA continued doling out bonuses. What's worse? Nearly half the bonuses in 2014 went to the same employees as the previous year, effectively rewarding its staff for the gratuitous deaths of thousands of American veterans. In 2016, the VA disclosed only $22 million worth of bonuses to 38,292 employees and continued to hide its 'performance bonuses.'

If veterans are dying because there are not

enough doctors to see them, the logical solution would be for the VA to hire more doctors. It is not that the VA isn't hiring *any* doctors – it is that they are hiring *so many* other employees in non-medical roles. From 2015 to 2016, the VA made 20,711 new hires; but just 2,091 were doctors, continuing the historical 10:1 doctor to non-doctor employee hiring ratio at the agency. In 2016, the VA had 372,614 total employees but just 8 percent of these were medical doctors, dental officers, optometrists, or podiatrists.

Even as the VA claims to be improving, treatment is still subpar for thousands of veterans. This year, the VA Secretary David Shulkin admitted that more than 90,000 disability claims would take more than 125 days to process. And over 500,000 veterans still wait longer than 30 days to even see a doctor. Why, then, does the VA continue to hire so many nonessential employees?

In 2016, the VA employed 3,498 police officers at a total cost of $172 million. All names and locations of these officers, however, were redacted. When asked about corresponding crime statistics, the VA was unable to provide any information on the number of crimes or incidents. Bear in mind that, as of 1996, the VA employed no police officers with arrest and firearm authority at all.

Today's officers not only draw large salaries, they're equipped with expensive and unnecessary equipment. In 2015, almost $2 million was spent on riot helmets, shields, body armor, a cannon system, tactical gear, and other equipment for crowd control. The average physician at the VA makes around $205,000 a year, meaning the VA could employ 840 doctors instead of 3,498 police officers. These doctors would help fulfill President Lincoln's promise to "care for him who shall have borne the battle." How, exactly, does an army of VA police officers help do that?

It is not just police officers that drive unnecessary costs at the VA. The VAs retains a large staff of nonessential, non-medical employees ranging from photographers to archaeologists. These employees regularly make six-figure salaries, diverting valuable funds away from the agency's core mission. Perhaps the most scandalous example is the stable of interior designers on the VA payroll. A total of 171 interior designers earned $50 million in salary and bonuses during the last four years. Most egregiously, the VA facility in Palo Alto, California, keeps nine interior designers on staff. In 2016, this very facility also spent $670,000 on sculptures to decorate the facility's exterior. The catch? This part of the Palo Alto facility serves blind veterans. Instead of pointless sculptures, the agency could have provided our veterans with three more doctors. The VA's wasted spending on art is only increasing. Between 2004 and 2007, the agency spent $1.5 million on art, while from 2008 to 2014 the artwork expenditures reached a towering $16.2 million dollars.

While this fiscal recklessness costs taxpayers their hard-earned dollars, it robs veterans of proper healthcare. Veteran Herb Whitlock suffers with a three-inch metal stint that was left in his nose following sinus surgery in 2011. He lives three-hundred miles from the nearest VA specialty clinic, but has been unable to gain approval to see a private specialist under "VA Choice Program Care." When he inquired as to why, his local VA administrators told him they "don't even know the qualifications for the Choice Program."

The VA's bloat has many human faces, including recent VA Secretary David Shulkin himself. Just this year (2018) it was revealed that Shulkin misspent taxpayer dollars during a European junket, costing the VA at least $122,000. A recent report by the Inspector General detailed Shulkin's "serious derelictions," including "improperly" paying for his

---

In 2016, over $20 million in grants were distributed to arts institutions with an asset base greater than $1 billion.

---

wife's travel and drafting a fellow VA employee to act as their "personal travel concierge" for the journey. Unbelievably, Shulkin also procured tickets to attend the women's finals match at Wimbledon – and lied about it to ethics officials.

PRESIDIO TRUST: WHERE SAN FRANCISCO BEGAN AND BONUSES CONTINUE

Properly administered, the VA plays important role in the lives of our veterans; and even the EPA can serve legitimate purposes. But the swamp is not solely composed of big government agencies the American public knows by name. And the swamp is not as clustered in and around Washington, D.C., as many might expect. We were astonished to learn the full reach of federal bureaucracy – and just how little service many of these lesser-known agencies provide the American public.

Take the Presidio Trust, a small federal agency created in 1996 to manage the San Francisco Presidio, a former military base which is now a public park. The Trust was tasked with managing this conversion process. According to its website, the Presidio is "where San Francisco began. Once a premier Army post, today the Presidio is a national park unlike any you have experienced before." Located at the south end of the Golden Gate Bridge, the Presidio holds property assets of over $400 million, all rented at market rate to generate revenue. The land managed by Presidio makes up 5 percent of San Francisco's land. Though the original creation of the agency was funded by taxpayer dollars, Presidio Trust became financially self-sufficient in 2013. Today, the Presidio runs completely on a revenue-generated surplus.

If the Presidio Trust sounds like a nonessential government agency, that is because it is.

Not only is the Presidio Trust useless, but we also discovered that it is one of the most galling sources of federal waste in the country. Despite a relatively small payroll of 326 employees, Presidio Trust granted three of the four largest federal bonuses in 2016.

Surely there are deserving federal employees who have worked hard to earn bonuses. But is Bart Ferrell one of them? The federal government awarded Ferrell, a human resources manager in charge of processing payroll at the Presidio Trust, an astounding $141,525 bonus, bringing his total compensation to $326,525. And in 2015, Ferrell received a $89,375 bonus – also one of the largest bonuses awarded by the federal government since 2014. Ferrell is not only an exceedingly well-paid member of the extended swamp network – he is a nearly permanent one. A profile of Ferrell on the Presidio Trust's website lists thirty years of experience, all at government agencies. Starting in the Peace Corps, Ferrell moved to the Department of Interior, the Treasury, and the General Services Administration. Ferrell's entire career has been spent swimming laps around the swamp, whether in D.C. or farther afield, and now he is receiving his supposedly just deserts.

And Ferrell is not an aberration. In fact, Presidio Trust awarded 6 out of the 10 largest federal bonuses from 2014 to 2016. Four of these bonuses exceeded $100,000, including a $147,000 bonus to Eileen Fanelli in 2014 for her position in "General Physical Science." That year, Fanelli's bonus was larger than her salary ($146,860). Other top Presidio Trust bonuses included $140,000 to Craig Middleton, a program manager; $126,218 to Karen Cook, a general attorney; and $80,330 to Francene Gonek, a realtor. Michael L. Boland received a $74,688 bonus as a "Miscellaneous Administration and Program" employee. In total, 7 in 10 of the agency's 326 employees received bonuses.

When asked about the department's pattern of awarding large bonuses, a spokeswoman from Presidio Trust issued the following response:

> *We are competing for talent in the Bay Area job market. Given the very high cost of living in the Bay Area, and the tight labor market, we make payments in addition to regular salary for the following reasons: signing, performance, retention and departure.*

Why is the Presidio Trust part of the federal government at all?

National Foundation on the Arts and Humanities: Art for Whose Sake?

While most would agree that the arts are a vital facet of a healthy culture, it is less certain that the government should be funding them. And when we looked into federally funded arts, the necessity of government funding became even more dubious.

The National Foundation on the Arts and Humanities (NFA-H) has a noble goal: "to develop and promote a broadly conceived national policy of support for the humanities and the arts in the United States, and for institutions which preserve the cultural heritage of the United States." The NFA-H is the umbrella organization over the National Endowment for the Humanities (NEH), which aims to "serve and strengthen our republic by promoting excellence in the humanities and conveying lessons of history to all Americans," and the National Endowment for the Arts (NEA), whose support gives Americans "the opportunity to participate in the arts, exercise their imaginations, and develop their creative capacities."

In 2016, these organizations collectively doled out $444.1 million in grants to 3,163 entities ranging from nonprofit organizations, to institutions of higher education, to other government entities, and to groups labeled "Indian Tribes" by the government. And yet despite the agencies' stated goals to serve *all* Americans, almost half of the grant dollars were clustered in just 10 states.

While these agencies and their missions sound worthy in principle, in practice they engage in funding behavior that most Americans would find difficult to stomach. Take, for instance, a $10,000 grant to a San Francisco–based organization called the Asian American Women Artists Association. The group mounted an exhibition, with NFA-H funds, to showcase the work of the late Yuri Kochiyama, a so-called civil rights activist who

In spite of these billions spent on PR, less than 20 percent of Americans trust the government to do what is right most of the time.

once declared, "I consider Osama bin Laden as one of the people I admire."

But it is not just small organizations like the Asian American Women Artists Association that benefit from the NFA-H largesse. Most of the grants distributed by the agency go to support organizations that have hardly any need at all. In 2016, over $20 million in grants were distributed to institutions with an asset base greater than $1 billion. Moreover, $105.9 million flowed to 1,077 nonprofit organizations with than $1 million in assets each. In fact, 80 cents on every dollar of NFA-H grants to non-profits and higher education went to organizations with assets greater than $1 million.

These asset-rich organizations can't claim they need the money. And neither can New York City's Metropolitan Museum of Art. Annually, the "Met Gala" benefit hosts "fashion's biggest night," a red-carpet fundraising event with rock stars such as Katy Perry, Pharrell Williams, and Madonna. Despite assets of $4 billion, the Met collected $1.2 million in federal grants from taxpayers since 2009. Why? Because they can.

After a careful review of NFA-H grants, it is clear that the grants tend to fall into two categories: those to large, well-funded organizations that have no clear need for federal money; and those to small, poorly funded organizations who do suspicious work. Take a $10,000 grant to the Borderlands Theater, a Tucson, Arizona, organization that describes its vision thusly:

Although focusing on the Latino / Chicano / Mexicano voice as the core voice to nurture and support, Borderlands works interactively with all voices of the region. The 'border,' both as physical and social landscape, is a metaphor for

Borderlands' work. The metaphor allows, invites and even demands, both a regional and an international understanding of what it represents. Border people, in the best sense of the word, are citizens of the world.

The NFA-H grant went to support a "series of site-responsive performances celebrating the saguaro cactus." The attendees were to sit or stand with a cactus for an hour in the desert. Participants were encouraged to see what they could learn from the cactus – and subsequently urged to share their experience on social media with the hashtag #IStand-WithSaguaros. But while the federal government might stand with saguaros, it is hard to believe that taxpayers would, if given the choice.

While some projects supported by the NFA-H border on the absurd, others appear to be motivated by the swamp's desire to push its political values on the public.

Take the New York Shakespeare Festival, which received has received some $30 million in taxpayer grants – federal, state, and local –

since 2009. In the summer of 2017 the organization staged a version of Shakespeare's *Julius Caesar* in which the titular character appears as a doppelgänger of President Trump and dies a bloody death. While the director Oskar Eustis basked in the approval of the beltway media, some theatergoers took issue with the unabashedly partisan nature of the show. Corporate sponsors such as Delta Airlines and Bank of America withdrew their support of the production, while American Express distanced itself.

The American public, unfortunately, does not have the luxury of withdrawing their support for artistic productions they find distasteful. The swamp – in this case, 432 NFA-H employees, earning $41.8 million in salary and bonuses annually – decides what art is good for them.

Facets of the Swamp

As the above examples have demonstrated, far from being confined to the carpeted corridors of Washington, D.C., the swamp is diffused throughout America. Federal bureaucrats are stationed in nearly 30,000 ZIP codes around the country, out of a total 43,000 or so. That means 70 percent of US ZIP codes contain federal employees.

And while federal salaries naturally have the power to shock, the federal government's widespread but largely unreported practice of distributing significant bonuses to its employees should be a major cause for alarm, too.

The federal government doled out $1.5 billion in bonuses in 2016, but disclosed just 330,000 bonuses totaling $351 million. Performance bonuses totaling nearly $1.1 billion were withheld due to anti-transparency language contained within government-union contracts. The U.S. Office of Personnel Management's official line on this lack of transparency is as follows:

"Because of agreements with federal employee unions we cannot release performance award amounts for individuals. Because performance awards are usually a percentage of an employee's annual salary which varies by performance

rating, someone could determine the employee's rating which is not releasable."

We do have some insight into these federal performance ratings, however, and it is, as you might expect, disturbing. A Government Accountability Office audit published last summer – using 2013 data – found that 99.6 percent of all federal workers received job performance ratings of "fully successful." As

---

Most Americans still choose to enter the private sector rather than become swamp-dwellers.

Don Devine, the director of the White House Office of Personnel Management during the Reagan administration, noted, that's a higher rating than the advertised purity of Ivory soap (99.3 percent).

When federal bureaucrats give themselves stratospheric job performance ratings like these, they fatten up their pay and bonus levels. That helps to explain the undisclosed $1.1 billion in performance bonuses the swamp and government unions don't want us to know about.

Currently, the federal government pays out five types of bonus: performance, incentive, recruitment, relocation, and retention bonuses. We argue that each of these types of bonuses should be subject to the Freedom of Information Act transparency law. So, we worked with Congressman Mark Sanford (SC-1) on the Federal Employee Bonus Disclosure Act of 2018 that would make performance bonuses subject to public disclosure.

On top of high salaries and big bonuses, federal employees enjoy luxurious benefits and paid time-off packages. On average, each federal worker receives 10 federal holidays, 13 sick days, and 20 vacation days. We estimate these benefits cost taxpayers $22.6 billion annually.

In addition to a wealth of holidays, sick days, and vacation days, federal employees are able to request more than 20 different types of paid leave including court leave, sick leave, annual leave, advanced sick leave, advanced annual leave, administrative leave, and more.

And benefits are not limited to time off. Federal employees receive a host of other perks that private-sector workers can only dream about, including child-care subsidies, commuter subsidies, federal student loan repayment programs up to $10,000 per year, retirement benefits, health insurance, life insurance, and telework. In 2016, roughly a quarter of federal employees telecommuted – with 17 percent of these telecommuting 3 or more days per week, 8.5 times the national average. While most Americans trudge to the office daily, federal employees do the bidding of the swamp in their pajamas.

To ensure the American people don't realize how the swamp exercises its pernicious influence over their lives, the federal government spends bundles of cash promoting itself in a positive light. In 2016, federal agencies poured $368.4 million into compensating in-house public relations and marketing personnel – that's $3.7 billion every ten years. On top of the in-house personnel costs, federal agencies spent billions of dollars on contracts with outside PR firms, as well. Some of these firms charge the agencies (taxpayers) $88 per hour for their interns and $525 per hour, or $1.1 million per year, for their executives. From 2007 to 2014, the feds spent $4.3 billion on public relations. In spite of these billions spent on PR, less than 20 percent of Americans trust the government to do what is right most of the time.

Operation Drain the Swamp

The swamp is deeper and more expansive than we could have imagined. But investigations by policymakers and engaged citizens will help uncover more corners that need cleaning up. If the Trump administration is serious about its campaign promise to "drain the swamp," it must make civil service reform a priority.

Indeed, in a 2017 *Wall Street Journal* editorial titled "A Big, Beautiful Trump 2018 Issue," columnist Kimberley Strassel identified a curtailing of the administrative state as both a worthy and characteristic goal for Trump and the Republicans in 2018. "Call it Operation Drain the Swamp," she wrote.

With control of both houses of Congress and the presidency, Republicans have a generational chance to rid Washington of its mephitic stench.

To work toward that goal, we recommend three action steps for civil service reform:

1. *Open the Books*

Some of the swamp is still murky – and you can't cut what you can't see. The first step to cleaning up the swamp is adding transparency where transparency is direly needed. It is time to shine a light on its true depths.

The largest swamp of opacity is the $125 billion in annual federal pension payout. Current law prohibits disclosure, claiming a violation of privacy for the federal employee. But taxpayers deserve to see all the details of the pensions their tax dollars are funding. Bringing transparency to federal pensions would require an act of Congress. So, we worked with Congressman Ron DeSantis (FL-6) on the Taxpayer Funded Pension Disclosure Act (H.R.3200) that would open the books on retirement annuities. Americans deserve to know the pension amount of retired IRS boss Lois Lerner, among many others. Congress should pass this bill, and soon.

Luckily, not all of the swamp is so opaque.

The last thing Americans need is to be sold on more government by the government itself. And yet this is exactly where a goodly portion of their federal tax dollars are going.

But even when making itself transparent, the bureaucracy does its best to hide its true reach. Out of nearly 2 million disclosed salary and award records in fiscal year 2016, there were 314,890 redacted names, including all 77,000 employees at the Internal Revenue Service (IRS). Additionally, there were 3,500 salaries redacted, including the Federal Reserve and the Consumer Financial Protection Bureau (CFPB).

In fiscal year 2017, it was worse. The Office of Personnel Management (OPM) redacted 255,000 federal salaries from the payroll data. Now, approximately 1 of every 5 federal salaries in the administrative agencies is withheld from the public, hiding an estimated $20 billion in payroll costs from the American people who foot the bill. These redactions didn't blackout secret positions at the CIA or other intelligence agencies, but rather staffers employed by regulatory, paper-pushing agencies. For example, OPM withheld the salaries of 51,000 "compliance inspectors and support staff" who work for the Transportation Security Administration (TSA). This means we can't see how much the TSA agents performing baggage checks and pat-downs at the airport are making. The feds redacted salaries of 7,500 miscellaneous program administrators, clerks, and assistants; 5,800 lawyers; and even innocuous positions such as 267 student trainees; 92 public affairs officers; and 62 photographers.

OPM even redacted more than 2,000 of their own employee salaries – that's nearly half of their internal workforce. It's a classic case of the bureaucracy protecting the bureaucracy, the swamp protecting the swamp.

In total, beyond the 2 million employees at the Department of Defense and in the active military, there's nearly $150 billion in undisclosed cash compensation per year: $1 billion in undisclosed bonuses, $125 billion in hidden pension payouts, and $20 billion in redacted salaries. Why should these employees and retirees receive the privilege of opacity? It is time to fully shine a light on the swamp.

2. *Downsize Rich Benefits Packages*

Working for the government is a sweet deal. According to a 2011 American Enterprise Institute study, federal salaries are 14 percent higher than their private-sector counterparts. Factor in benefits and compensation premiums and the difference jumps to an astonishing 61 percent. That is because federal employees receive big bonuses, plentiful paid time off, cushy pensions, and union protections. It is a testament to the federal government's inherent noxiousness that even with the obvious benefits of a government position, most Americans still choose to enter the private sector rather than become swamp-dwellers.

The U.S. government hands out $1.5 billion in bonuses every year. Paying bonuses to public employees is problematic, adding huge costs to the already massive federal payroll. The bonus program should be cut entirely from federal payroll practices.

Federal employees who make it three years

in their government position are eligible for 8.5 weeks of paid time off including 10 federal holidays, 13 sick days, and 20 days of vacation time. We estimate that these generous paid time off allowances cost taxpayers $23 billion annually. Cutting the package by just 25 percent would still allow for ample time off – six whole weeks, 20 more days than the average American – and would lessen the taxpayer burden by $6.3 billion.

3. *Cut Frivolous Positions*

The cavalcade of federal jobs includes valiant positions like "Medical Officer" and "Police." But must the federal government have on its books employees tasked with "Book Binding" and "Wood Crafting"?

This morass of workers makes up an agonizingly expensive bureaucracy. The Trump administration should cut frivolous positions with vigor. There are more than 3,600 public affairs and marketing employees stationed across 70 federal departments and independent agencies. These in-house agents of self-promotion cost taxpayers $368 million annually on top of the billions of dollars the federal government spends on PR contracts with outside firms. The last thing Americans need is to be sold on more government by the government itself. And yet this is exactly where a goodly portion of their federal tax dollars are going.

There are 120,000 program officers, analysts and their bosses with salaries costing the American taxpayer over $12 billion per year. These are the folks administering federal programs. Does the Small Business Administration (SBA) really need to give $200 million in low-cost, taxpayer backed loans to golf, swim, tennis, and country clubs? How about the $25 billion in federal grants to the eight colleges of the Ivy League during a six-year period? What about tens of millions of dollars in farm subsidies flowing into major American cities – where there are no farms?

The federal payroll includes hundreds of interior designers for a $22 million annual tab, photographers making up to $158,000, and laundry and food service employees making six-figure salaries. Even allowing for the fact that some of these employees might provide essential services, there's still plenty of space to eliminate needless – and expensive – positions. Trust us, the American people won't miss the professional photographs of every ribbon-cutting ceremony.

THE TIME IS NOW

It has been 40 years since the last civil service overhaul, and it is time for a united push by politicians to scale down the administrative state. Far from being the hobby horse of a few libertarian radicals, swamp draining should be a bipartisan issue centered on accountability, fairness, and appropriate spending.

The task is daunting. It is worth repeating Ronald Reagan's 1983 observation that "sometimes it's difficult to remember that you didn't send us to Washington to feed the alligators, you sent us to drain the swamp." President Trump, in making swamp-draining a major plank of his 2016 campaign policy platform, appears to understand this intuitively. Taxpayers are rightly concerned about high salaries, lucrative benefit packages, excessive bonuses, and cushy retirement pensions.

Far from being the hobby horse of a few libertarian radicals, swamp draining should be a bipartisan issue centered on accountability, fairness, and appropriate spending.

With the American people, the sitting president, and both houses of Congress all in support of curtailing the power and reach of the federal government, the time is now. The swamp must be drained before it drags every aspect of American life into its ever-expanding muck.

Thomas W. Smith
Chairman of OpenTheBooks.com

Dr. Tom Coburn
Honorary Chairman

Adam Andrzejewski
CEO & Founder and author of this publication

Acknowledgements

Mr. Thomas W. Smith, our Chairman at OpenTheBooks.com, for his organizational guidance, personal wisdom, and generous support of our mission. Jessie Fox, Communications Specialist, for her impactful work drafting and editing this publication. Craig Mijares, Chief Operating Officer, and Aran Spence, Director of Information Technology, for capturing the data and literally mapping 2 million federal civil service employees by employer ZIP code. Frank Bruno, Director of Government Oversight, for the research necessary to compile our original 'Mapping The Swamp' oversight report on which this broadside publication is built. Matthew Tyr-mand, Deputy Director at Large, for his advice, counsel, and influential network of media, political and NGO contacts using our oversight findings as the motivation to create real change.

We also want to acknowledge Ben Riley, the associate editor of *The New Criterion* and Sam Schneider, marketing director at Encounter Books, for their individual impacts on this publication. The editors helped us curate, edit, and finalize our many stories of federal government abuse, fraud, corruption and taxpayer abuse. We are grateful for their assistance.

This report quantifies federal transactions compiled at www.OpenTheBooks.com as a result of the Federal Funding Accountability and Transparency Act of 2006. To the extent the government makes mistakes in reporting inaccurate or incomplete data, our publication will reflect these same mistakes.

Today, OpenTheBooks.com is the largest private repository of U.S. public-sector spending. With Honorary Chairman Dr. Tom Coburn, the group has one ultimate goal: post "every dime, online, in real time." To date, OpenThe-Books.com has captured 4 billion government-spending records, including 16 million public employee salary and pension records across America; nearly all disclosed federal government spending since 2000; and 47 of 50 state checkbooks.

OpenTheBooks.com exposed the $20 million luxury-art procurement program at the Department of Veterans Affairs, which forced a public apology from the V.A. Secretary and the adoption of new rules to stop the abuse (2016). The group found 63,000 highly compensated Illinois public employees earned $100,000+ costing taxpayers $10 billion (2017). Recently, OpenTheBooks launched *Mapping The Swamp* – an interactive mapping platform displaying 2 million federal bureaucrats by employer ZIP code across America.

OpenTheBooks.com is harnessing three powerful forces in the internet age: the power of the Freedom of Information Act (FOIA); the latest in big data technology; and the ability to follow the money using forensic auditing techniques.

The group's oversight model has led to the assembly of grand juries, indictments, successful prosecutions, congressional briefings and hearings, subpoenas, and Government Accountability Office (GAO) audits, administrative policy changes, federal legislation, and much more.

© 2018 by American Transparency

All rights reserved. No part of this publication may be reproduced, stored in a retrieval system, or transmitted, in any form or by any means, electronic, mechanical, photocopying, recording, or otherwise, without the prior written permission of Encounter Books, 900 Broadway, Suite 601, New York, New York, 10003.

First American edition published in 2018 by Encounter Books, an activity of Encounter for Culture and Education, Inc., a nonprofit, tax exempt corporation. Encounter Books website address: www.encounterbooks.com

Manufactured in the United States and printed on acid-free paper. The paper used in this publication meets the minimum requirements of ANSI / NISO z39.48–1992 (R 1997) (*Permanence of Paper*).

FIRST AMERICAN EDITION

LIBRARY OF CONGRESS CATALOGING-IN-PUBLICATION DATA IS AVAILABLE

Andrzejewski, Adam
Operation drain the swamp / Adam Andrzejewski.
pages cm. , (Encounter broadsides ; 56)
ISBN 978-1-64177-029-3 (pbk. : alk. paper) —
ISBN 978-1-64177-030-9 (ebook)

10 9 8 7 6 5 4 3 2 1

SERIES DESIGN BY CARL W. SCARBROUGH